Dancing on the

Beach

Cathy Teoste

DEDICATION

This book is dedicated to my daughters,
Nicole, Samantha and Monica
As they set sailing on their own life journeys,
told me to go have my own adventure.
And to all those who have danced with me
along the way.

ACKNOWLEDGMENTS

I have had a great deal of support and encouragement along the way to Dancing on the Beach.

To those in the Wisconsin woods who sheltered me and provide the soil for me to regain my strength and rebuild my core foundation.

A special thank you to Sr. Henrita who told me to "Dream Big', to Raymundo and Roberta for reawakening my love of dance, to Linda and John for their encouragement and support in becoming myself.

To the people both residents and visitors of Topsail Island who welcomed and befriended me as I arrived home at the Atlantic Ocean.

To my Mermaid Sister Cindy who suggested I needed to write this book, Thank-you for your assistance and encouragement

A Special Thank You to my friends and editors, Bruce and Patti who took care of me every day as I wrote this book and danced on the beach and knew the words to the songs I needed to match the steps of my Dance.

Table of Contents

Preface

Through this collection of essays, I express my deep love and connection to the ocean and with my own inner spirit. I hope to inspire you to connect with nature and your own authentic essence, hear your own deep inner wisdom, discover your own song in your heart and dance the steps to your own unique dance fully embracing life in all of its wonder and awe.

Through these essays you will:

- Become centered in present moment
- Connect to nature and your inner spirit
- Awaken your senses, learning to experience life through all your senses in every moment
- Experience the wonders of beauty and awe, the colors of the rainbow and all the world has to offer
- Tune into what is right for you now
- Open your heart to new ways of seeing, thinking, doing and being
- Hear your own inner voice deepening and expanding your vision, shifting and

gaining a new perspective of yourself
and of life

Combining contemplation with action you will,

- Hear and dance to your own tune
- Shed your inhibitions tossing them into the wind and waves
- Move to the rhythm of the waves and your own inner song acting boldly towards what attracts you and what brings you joy
- Discover a new way of being and acting in the world in alignment with your authentic self
- Express your true essence being fully present in your life and have confidence to dance beyond the breakers
- Awaken your love for life itself

The wisdom of your heart comes from the lessons of nature and takes wings in your creative expression.

When you show up in the world in a way that is genuine and true to who you really are, your world will shift and change in the most amazing ways.

The wisdom of the beach has guided me into my own inner wisdom found deep in my heart and soul and leading me to learn to hear the song of my own soul and the steps of my own joy.

I am now learning to dance beyond the breakers.

My wish for you is that you discover your own deep inner wisdom and joy Discovering the step to the dance within your own heart.

Introduction

I have always felt the call of the ocean but I was never able to answer it. I have always felt like a fish living out of the water. I never quite fit in on the landlocked world. For many years I lived in the woods and the mountains. The lakes, rivers and streams kept me alive when I was barely breathing but they never truly nourished me. It never felt like home. Their energy and beauty gave me hope while reminding me that water was my substance.

If one believes in astrology then it makes sense that I am so at home at the sea. I am a Pisces, the two fish swimming in opposite directions, one swimming with the current and the other against the current. This sums up my life in simple terms. I grew up with two distinct parts of myself in conflict with each other.

When I arrived on this island I knew I had found home even though it was far away from everyone and everything I had ever known. I met a woman who, after speaking with me for a few minutes, recognized me as a Sister Mermaid. I had never thought of myself as a Mermaid before but it fit. Suddenly my whole life fell into place.

The ocean is my soul. It gives me peace. It touches my heart. It gives me love. It gives me joy. It gives me hope. It gives me life. I am blessed and graced because of it. I am grateful for the abundance it brings to me, for the substance and nourishment that it provides me.

Now that I am living at the ocean, privileged to be able to come and visit with her every day, I have been changed. She has transformed me in ways no one can see on the outside. On the inside, however, she has shifted my consciousness and my heart in ways I never imaged….never believed I was capable of…

I can never be the same again. Old ways have been shed and new ways are unfolding as the ocean continues to come and go bringing in new treasures and taking away things I no longer need. I can never again live without being near her.

People who know the ocean as I do call it beautiful or amazing….I just call it mine…my home. You are welcome to make it yours as well. There is more than enough to share.

The ocean with her magnificent waves, her depth and expansiveness out to the horizon is my home. It is where I belong.

This book has come out of my love of the ocean, the beach and dancing. It is how my heart sings. It is a collection of stories, pieces of my life and how I connect them to the ocean and the expression of my emotions and circumstances.

I will try to describe all of what I see, hear, and feel in words, but the deep connection of my spirit with the ocean, all the different ways I feel connected to the ocean, can best be understood through your own experience.

In this book, I hope to give you a glimpse of what I experience. Better yet, I hope to inspire you to create an expression of your inner self and let it out into the world.

The Inspiration

The Ocean

I live on an island, no matter how good or bad the day is, I get to see the magnificent ocean.

The waves lull me into the present moment….into stillness. I am in awe of her beauty.

My senses come alive. I see clearly. I hear the songs of the waves. I smell each scent that blows on the wind. I taste the water and the air. I feel the particles of sand on my feet and particles of water and salt on my skin.

Life is determined in the present moment and its glory is in the details. The different colors of the ocean can change in an instant. It shifts and changes with the light right before my eyes. The colors can range between a grey green to glistening blue with white dancing dots to hundreds of shades not just green and blue but purple, pink, brown and black. It is diverse from shore to horizon in any given moment. I might miss it if I am not paying attention.

The ocean brings her energy to me and she revives me. I slip into a peaceful state of relaxation where all my cares and woes drift out to sea.

It is where I go to be alone to connect to nature, to myself, to life, to God. It is where God is for me. I am drawn to this place. It calls to me. I hear the sound of the waves no matter where I am and I must go to her.

The ocean is where I go to pray when my life has hit some crisis or a brick wall or is just stale or I am stuck.

The ocean reaches into my weakest moments and reminds that I am strong.

Here seeing her magnificence I feel and express my gratitude. Everything is right, I recognize the good that has happened in my life. It makes any day a good day.

Here I look out over her surface to the horizon and stand on the horizon of myself, my hopes and dreams. My life is contained within the depths of her.

My connection to the ocean is where I connect to myself. Here is where I really go inside myself, into my heart, into my soul.

Nature is one ingredient to a happy state of mind, emotional well-being and mental energy. The rewards and effects can continue long after you return to your day to day life.

Exposure to the ocean eases us into feelings of relaxation and security, our blood pressure drops, stress eases away. The sounds of the ocean calms our emotions, triggers deep memories, and activates self-reflection. It helps put our self and our life in perspective as we look out to the horizon and realize the depths of the ocean itself.

The Beach

The beach is the in-between place between the ocean and the land. It is where transition and change take place. It is a sacred space of healing and comfort. Here on the beach, I can experience all of the shades of life and self.

I sit on the beach and dream. I listen to the wisdom of the sea...so many lessons to learn....so many joys to experience...so much beauty to see. It is all here to savor.

The beach is where I have contemplated life, my life, where I have been, where I am going.

I come here with my confusion and a restless spirit, disconnected and broken. I come here with all of my faults, my inadequacies, my regrets, my sadness, my heartache. I give them all to the sea, tossing them into the wind and into the waves.

I come here with my joy and happiness. I come here with my gratitude and love. I come here with abundance to share. It is the cradle that allows me to experience the ocean.

Here on the beach everything comes together. I never know what I will find on the beach. I may be alone and find myself basking in stillness and serenity. I may find connection and friendship with others. I may find playfulness and fun. I may find a storm brewing off shore, racing towards me.

The sand has emotional power all its own. It is impressionable, mutable and impermanent. It opens the doors of the unconscious and awakens our creativity. Building sandcastles or creating a master piece knowing we can change it easily. Aware that the ocean will wash it away eventually.

On the beach you can shift with the tides through changes of yourself and your life. You can contemplate how you want to be, who you want to become and how your life will expand. You can try out new possibilities in the sand.

As the landscape of the beach is changed by the tides of the sea I am changed by my experiences of the beach.

Here on the beach Transition and vision merge together. Laugh, play, sing, dance, and express your inner child and your truest deepest self. Just be and see what the tides bring to your feet.

What wonders and possibilities and treasures are here for you. What might you discover?

The Dance

Life is a Dance. Life is in constant movement.
We are in constant movement. We move
through phases, transitions and situations.
Sometimes we know the steps and sometime
we make them up, improvising as we go along.

My dance has had many missteps and many
times when I clearly didn't know the steps.
What I have learned is that I don't need or
want to dance the steps of other people's
dances. I want to create my own dance. I have
wasted too much of my life trying to learn the
steps of everyone else's dances. I have been
held back by the rigidity of a set pattern of
steps. It was fine to learn a variety of steps
but I don't need to do them in the same
structure and pattern as anyone else.

Now that I know the basic steps I need to put
them together in a way that sings from my
soul. And I need to make up a few of my own
moves too!

I need to Just Be Me.

*When I hear the music of the ocean my feet
have to jump and move for joy. When I see
dolphins frolicking in the sea, I must join them.
Dancing is the expression of my passion for the
ocean*

Learn the basic steps but make up your own dance and add a touch of your own steps to make your heart sing.

It takes courage and practice to learn the steps to your own dance. It takes stillness, reflection and contemplation. You must hear and listen deeply to your soul.

Nature gives us the opening to guide us into those places deep within us we must listen to in order to hear the whispers of our heart and the music of our soul.

Step out onto the beach. Walk down beside the water. Stand still. Listen to the sounds around you. Let the sounds around you lead you within.

Listen to the wave's roar, their rhythmic pattern, regular and irregular, the sounds they make as they lap upon the shore.

Sit upon the sand. Look out over the horizon. Go within. Listen carefully. What is the ocean saying to you? What is the wind whispering in your ear?

Now go deeper into your heart. It has something important to say to you. Listen. Your heart is beating steadily. It has its own rhythm. That is part of your tune.

Listen to the sounds of your body. They are humming a tune.

Listen to your soul. It is wanting to connect with you and tell you its secrets. It is singing your tune. The song that is yours and yours alone.

Hear it?

Get up and begin to move. Listen to the sounds of nature. Move in any way that feels comfortable. Walk, Walk into the water. Splash your feet. Skip, Hop. Whatever movements your body wants to make.

Now go deeper add the sounds of your heart. Begin to express those heart felt desires. Relax into it. Maybe now you are combining some dance and yoga moves or just jumping around splashing in the water.

Now go deeper and add the music your soul is singing to you. Let go of any inhibitions. Be completely present with yourself, body, mind and spirit. Let it soar. Dance like no one is watching!

Keep going until your spirit is free and you are dancing beyond the breakers!

And if you want to sing or laugh or yell - Go for it!

Dance to Your Own Song!

And Remember to listen to your heart and change the steps as you move through your life.

Create New Steps as you go along.

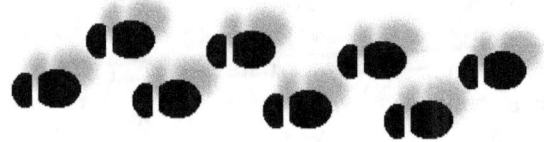

The Dance is Your Dance. How you move through life expresses who you are and how you feel about yourself and your life. Dancing is the creative expression of how you feel.

Take Your Dance Out into the World. Be an Authentic Self-Expression of Who You Are!

Dancing on the

Beach

Dancing in the Sand

Some days I just need to be outside. I need to feel my connection to the earth. I need to be barefoot in the sand, to feel it under my feet.

Soft sand lets me dig my feet in and warms me. Hard wet sand puts a foundation under my feet and cools me. I am grounded.

Sand greets the ocean as she reaches the shore. She cradles the shells and other items that spill from the ocean depths. The dunes protect the inland from the ocean when she threatens to spill from her bed.

I hear so many people complain about the sand. They hate how it feels on their skin and how it gets into everything. But sand is part of the deal if you love the beach. You must make peace with it.

Playing in the sand, shifting it between my fingers, molding it into different forms awakens my creativity. Mutable and impermanent I can try out different forms, creating and recreating as I please. Whatever I create I can knock it down myself or watch as it disappears into the ocean.

Beauty can be created. Creations can be dissolved into the sea. It reminds me that nothing lasts forever except the experience left as a memory.

As I go through my life I make imprints in the sand. Eventually they are washed away as I continue to make imprints in the sand. Those imprints can be light and soft or hard and wet. Life's steps can be a slow hard walk at times, with sadness and tears or light and free, with smiles and laughter. I can chose how I make those imprints either stomping or running through the sand, or strolling or dancing down the beach.

My feet move in the sand as I dance. It sometimes shifts and knocks me off balance but it is the foundation under my feet. It catches each step, even a misstep. It shifts and moves but is constantly under my feet supporting me as I move through each step of life.

Create your imprints that you leave behind in your experiences and the memories Focus on the steps you are making at this moment, they are what matter because the ones behind us are vanishing into the ocean of our life.

Dancing in the sand is one of foundation and balance. It is one of missteps and shifts. It is warm and hard, dry and wet. It is one of stability and steadfastness as well as unsteadiness. It is one of forming the groundwork, establishing your sense of self.

Dancing to the Sunrise

I awake every morning with my need to see
the ocean. I am pulled to it.

I cannot begin to function without breathing it
in through all of my senses. I anxiously head
to the beach to be drawn into the breath of
life.

I stand on the crossover and look out over the
ocean, scanning the horizon and take a deep
breathe.

The sun begins to show itself, slowly inching
about the horizon. This is the most gratifying
moment of the day.

I stand in reverence. Moments of meditation
watching the sun rise from beneath the ocean
to sit upon the horizon. A ball of brilliance.
Magnificent in her glory of color, red, orange,
yellow against the dark blue sea and the light
blue sky.

A new day, full of promise. No matter what
happened yesterday, I can start fresh again
today. I walk down onto the beach.

As I walk towards the ocean she comes up and
greets me. "Good Morning" I say as the ocean
washes over my toes and the sunlight shines
over me.

I open my arms to receive the energy of the sun and the ocean. I reach up and pull the sun's energy towards my body. Bringing my arms down towards the ocean I scoop her energy to me.

The ocean and sun are true and consistent friends. She allows and encourages me to face the day no matter what it may bring.

Everything I need is contained right here in this moment. Life is formed from her, lived in her, dies with her. This is where God exists for me. I begin to move.

This Dance is a slow dance….a dance of greeting and new beginnings…. stillness and peace. Taking the first steps. Just get going. Move your feet and enter into the dance and open into the possibilities of this day.

Dancing in the Sunshine

I am in awe of the colors of the ocean as the light of the sun sparkles through the water, illuminating it. I can feel the energy dancing off the surface of the ocean. If only I could harness it and learn how to use it.

Dancing in the sunlight I shine. The sun is my spotlight and I am the star. I am reminded to let my own unique light shine through.

Dare to be different. Dare to be myself. My significance is not determined by what I do for a living or how much money I make but by who I am, the kind of person I am and how I choose to live my life.

I choose to live my life in Joy. To inspire and be a source of inspiration to others. I express this though *Dancing on the Beach*. The Dance is my own unique creative expression of myself, my gratitude, my joy. My light shines through me to others when I am in my light.

This is a dance of energy and enthusiastic movement...jumping, spinning, and laughing. It is lively and intense. I am eager to accomplish and achieve all I set out to do. It is full of zest and brightness. It illuminates the very core of who I am. I am visible and seen in all aspects and dimensions of myself.

Dance in your own spot light- Let your inner light shine through your own unique creative expression.

Dancing to the Sunset

The sun continues to shine down on every part of my island as it moves across the sky. The afternoon wanes into evening. The blue color of the ocean changes shades and hues. The sun begins to add its own shades of pink and purple to the sky.

It is time to slow down. The day is ending. It is time to rest. To set aside time to reflect, see the beauty and be grateful for all that has transpired.

Sunset is a time of reflection and contemplation. It is one of both endings and beginnings. For in ending the day we embark upon a time of dreaming and visioning new beginnings...new paths to take, new hopes for the future.

I remember the steps of each dance I did this day, and dream of steps I wish to take tomorrow. I flow into each step with beauty and grace. I envision a new dawn after a peaceful rest.

As I began the day in stillness, I end the day in stillness. The dance ends for today.

This Dance is a dance of gratitude for all the beauty within the day. The steps slow down taking us easily into the night of dreams in restful sleep. It is one of meditation and peacefulness, ending in rest and restoration.

Dancing in the Wind

The wind can be a gentle sea breeze or a
strong north wind that creates a sandstorm on
the beach. It can change direction suddenly,
blowing everything in every direction at once.

Changes in our life are often like that.
Sometimes they come in softly, allowing us to
adjust easily and other times they come in so
strong they knock us down.

I breathe in the salt air. I feel the breeze swirl
though me and I shiver. I smell a mix of winter
and spring dancing with each other. I want to
dance for the end of winter and the beginning
of spring.

Sometimes it seems like winter just won't let
go and allow spring to blossom into being.
Spring has not generated enough warmth yet
to overpower the winter chill.

It is a pattern of steps that winter and spring
must dance until spring emerges in triumph.
There is nothing I can do to hurry it along.

Dancing in the wind is both alive with
movement and difficult to move in. Sometimes
I can jump into the wind and let it take me
anywhere. I don't need any effort in it. Other
times it is like climbing a mountain as I strain
for every step and breath.

Our life dance contains both times when we can sail to our destination easily with the wind at our back and times when we must work our sails to use the wind to our advantage. The wind can insist we use all our strength and determination to reach our destination. The wind takes us where we want to go or battles us every step of the way.

And sometimes you just need to change letting the wind take us off in a new direction. You might just find something better than you were looking for to begin with.

This Dance is full of energy and transformation. Quick and alive with continual movement. It changes course, spins, and turns. We can go with the flow and let it guide us or we can work with it to sail into our dreams.

Dancing with the Tides

The ocean slides up to my toes and greets me. I thank her for coming to welcome me. I stand and stare out to the horizon.

I watch the sea recede away from me, the stretch of beach between me and the ocean is growing larger and larger. The water is moving farther and farther away from me.

For many years I watched people leave my life and go off to explore the seas while I stayed in the same place. Now I am the one who has receded from my life to this ocean shore. As long as the ocean is here beside me I am not alone.

When I dance at low tide I have an expansive beach and plenty of room to move around and lots of space to skip and dance. I look deeply into the tide pools hoping to see something, but what do I expect to see?

When I dance at ebb tide the water always stays in the same spot as the ocean turns itself around. Ebb tide reassures me that there is always a pause in-between change. It reminds me to pause during the business of life.

Despite having little to no room to dance at high tide, I love dancing at high tide. The ocean is right at my feet. I can even dance in the water and kick it and splash it as I move

into and out of it. Life is full to the brim when I
dance at high tide.

Dancing with the tides is a dance of comings
and goings, old things leaving my life and new
things coming into my life. No matter how
much things change the essential things are
constant. Constant as the tides coming in and
going out.

*This Dance is one of consistency through
change. It requires modification and
adjustment, timing and scheduling. We move
forward and back, side to side sometimes
stagnant. Our steps must move in time with the
tides of the moment, the phases of our life.*

Dancing in the Waves

The ocean gives me life. I live because of her. I am one with the ocean. It is here that I must be. I can never get enough.

I can sit staring into the waves all day long. The rising and cresting and falling of the waves movement mesmerizes me. I am in a daze, in a trance empty of mind and lost in the depths of her.

Present moment is all there is.

I let the waves lap upon my feet and she soothes me. I long to slip into her embrace, she comforts me.

The waves challenge me to overcome my fears and walk through them or dive into them. I dance with them and through them. I become brave. My courage makes me strong.

The ocean waves always take me back to shore if I resist fighting the current. I learn to trust the earth and myself. Trust in yourself to ride the waves of life, the ups and downs and the challenges.

I ride each wave up and down and she relaxes me, releasing all my stress, restlessness. I am relaxed and alert at the same time.

I know now that I can take risks but also know when to relax and let the ups and downs of life take me gently to shore.

I am reconnected to the earth and to myself. My body has become entrained in the 'earth's breathing'. Just being and experiencing the cradle of life. I have returned to myself, to my being, to the natural world, to the inner rhythms of life.

This Dance begins in present moment, walks through fear and relaxes into peaceful movement. It is playful, fearless and serene. Dance connecting with the rhythm of the waves, with the movement of the ocean and the inner being of yourself.

Dancing with the Dolphins

As I swim in the waves I realize that the dolphins are there in front of me. I stop, afraid that I might scare them away, but they aren't bothered by me. Tentatively I reach out to touch them but it is I who am more afraid of them then they are of me. Swimming with wild dolphins... incredible and remarkable.

Dolphins all around me. My excitement rises. I watch a dolphin jump out of the ocean and splash playfully. They seem to be laughing as they ride the waves. I cannot help but feel playful jumping up and down in delight. I am playing in the waves with the dolphins along side of me. I am in heaven with all of God's creatures. I am finding fun once again.

Playfulness is an important part of retaining who we are. If we lose our ability to laugh and play we lose our creativity and imagination that bring magic and wonder into our life.

Each time I see a dolphin it is magical. Life is magical. More importantly, I feel safe and protected. I know that dolphins keep the sharks away. I know they would protect me from one if it came my way. Dolphins are gentle and kind animals but they can kill a shark and will defend you from it if need be.

Dolphins are social creatures. They interact and play with each other and travel together. I listen to them communicating with clicks to each other as they jump and ride the waves. I wonder what they are saying to each other and what they might say to me.

I want to share this fun with friends. I realize how important social contact and interaction is to my sense of self. It is an important part of life to share experiences together. I am beginning to understand why connection with others is so important to me.

If I understand this will it help to dissipate my fear of being alone? For I never am truly alone when I have the sea beside me.

This Dance is one of fun, playfulness and delight. The steps are light, magical, silly, teasing and mischievous. The steps intermingle with other's steps, connecting to and dancing with each other.

Dancing on an Empty Beach

On this day I am all alone on the beach doing some yoga. I begin to flow the movements together. I throw in a few ballet movements and I am dancing.

It is just me and the sand and the ocean. I let my spirit flow out of me. I lose myself in the movement. I am one with my body with my spirit in control.

I am free. This taste of freedom ignites a flame that I will not be able to put out.

For most of my life I have hated being alone. I have been afraid of being alone. Out of that moment of aloneness, of solitude, my spirit burst free. My passion became creative expression.

Dancing on the Beach was born in that moment.

One could say it could happen anywhere. For you the place may be different, the woods, a meadow, a studio, your bedroom. For me it is the ocean.

I am living both my dream, living at the ocean, and my nightmare, living alone. I can awaken each morning from the nightmare and know that it is just a dream, a creation of my imagination and not the reality of me.

Aloneness has given me freedom to be myself, to make my own choices, to do what is in my heart. I have no one to answer to but myself.

It is often in our darkest moments, in the depths of despair when our hearts and souls come forward to show us who we truly are.

This Dance is free, passionate, a true expression of one's heart and spirit not influenced by what others think. Listen to your inner voice, listen to your heart, Let go, Set your Spirit Free, Dance with passion, Express Yourself, Be Yourself. We should always dance as if no one is watching.

Dancing on a Crowded Beach

I never imagined I would be dancing on the beach. I have always been too shy to do anything in public. In fact, most of my life I have been afraid of my own shadow, of myself. All my dancing I did behind closed doors too worried about what people would think of me if they knew the person I hid inside.

I shut myself off from life. I began living on the sidelines, never engaged fully in life. I kept my self-expression imprisoned behind four walls. Alone in the privacy of my own room I could write and dance away the pain, sadness, hurt, and shame...let my imagination roam, release my feelings, liberate my passions. I never wanted anyone to see all this expression of emotions and movement I had inside of me.

I kept my true self hidden from myself and the world. Afraid of rejection and judgment. But I was not living. My soul began tugging at me. It wanted to break free. The ocean called to me and I answered her call. She healed me and nurtured my spirit forward.

The ocean inspired me to move with the sound and rhythm of the waves. But it is not enough to keep it to myself. I must be of service to others. I must be a source of inspiration. I must share my spirit and share my joy with others.

I love dancing on the beach. It is a true expression of my passion, my spirit and my being. It is who I am. I no longer care if I am that crazy lady who dances on the beach. If someone laughs or someone smiles then I have passed a bit of my joy to them and even if they are laughing at me instead of with me that is okay, at least they laughed today.

This Dance is one of shedding inhibitions, while having compassion and respect for others as I express myself. Don't let other people hold you back, or determine who you are or how you express yourself in the world. Dare to be yourself and have compassion for those who are afraid to dance to their own music.

Dancing in the Moonlight

The moon in the darkness shines her light across the ocean, illuminating just a single line. I drift in the sound of the waves into the empty space of No Mind. I am transported to a place where time and the world do not exist, where I am surrounded by Angels.

The ocean's sheer expansiveness overwhelms me. I wonder what is out there. I know that she reaches far beyond my sight and goes further than I can see.

I connect to the life force. I enter into the secret place. The internal wilderness of who I really am. One experience emerged from many. I know that if it was not for the darkness, the moon would not shine so brightly. It would not illuminate a path for me to follow.

What we cannot see is a mystery. Yet the moonlight makes it magical. I stand in the heart of my spirit. Everything is possible. I don't need to see everything, know everything. The light will shine upon what I need to know and see and my heart will lead the way.

Here, in the moonlight on the beach with the ocean in front of me, the two parts of myself become whole. I am one with myself, with the ocean, with the sand, with the earth, with the sky, with all of life, with the universe and with eternity.

This Dance is flowing, mystical, mysterious. It is deeply rooted from within. It moves in and out of the moonlight. Be surprised when the ocean touches your feet. It delights. The darkness within shows the light of the soul. Know and experience all of yourself in the moonlight. The moonlight dances with you as you dance in your own spotlight.

Dancing Under the Stars

Under the stars is where I can see the abundance of possibilities, where my imagination comes alive with dreams. Hope and faith flood my being. My spirit is woven from it. Hope falls from the stars into the sea and washes up at my feet.

The sky is filled with so many wonders. It sparkles, heaven on earth. Twinkling glowing lights litter the sky above. One only has to reach out and touch the sky and pull a dream down to earth. Imagine the dream, believe in it, and it will manifest when you wake.

As children we dream all kinds of dreams. As we grow older we believe that dreams are not real, that they are not valid. We squash our dreams. We must bring them back again.

Dreaming is the origin of creativity. Be open to all possibilities and opportunities. Believe in yourself as perfect just the way you are.

This Dance is one of hope and faith. It forms from knowing that all is possible. Believe in yourself….Dream Big….Grab a star…Wish upon it. The steps are light, bold, exciting yet filled with serenity. There is nothing to fear so let the imagination go and follow it where it leads you along the beach into the water….Dancing until it ends with you lying in the sand looking up at the sky that seems to fall into the ocean.

Dancing through a Storm

White caps rise and form randomly across the surface of the ocean like musical notes bouncing up and down. The song she is singing is fast and furious, full of anger and power, tossing and turning everything it gets hold of onto the beach.

It suits me, as I feel as volatile as the ocean's display. Unsettled....anxiety bubbling under the surface....I try hard to calm my body, my thoughts,...If you could see inside me you would see exactly what the ocean looks like today. She has me tossing and turning with her turbulence.

The ocean can be powerful. Storms can cause her to flood over everything outside her space. Her intensity can be life altering. Her strength forces me to take notice and be prepared to take cover and ride out the storm or even evacuate.

And yet I love storms. They give me energy. They excite me releasing enthusiasm I have kept inside. I feel alive. I am not afraid. I welcome the unpredictability of what may happen. There is nothing like watching a storm at sea. It is amazing, powerful, and life changing.

My life and the ocean are intertwined and intermingled. Our stories are the same. My life is her life and her life is my life...for the ocean is in me and I am in her.

This Dance is one of power, energy and intensity. It erupts from the soul. It is impulsive and strong. The body stays centered and strong while the arms and legs may move feverishly about, waving and kicking. It rushes with excitement, anticipation and energy. In the middle is the calm, the center, the stability. And when it is over we have mastered strength, courage and compassion.

Dancing on Seashells
& Stones and other debris

The ocean is dark blue, not winter blue but the blue of a storm just passed. The sand is covered with shells, stones and other debris.

All kinds of objects broken and forlorn…. My stomach is in knots and butterflies. My body is shaking not from the cold which is chilling my skin but from my fears and worries, all the obstacles that appear to be in my path. It seems anxiety is sitting on the edge of the horizon waiting to come in and take hold.

Each step I take must be taken carefully or my feet will be hurt. Yet if I walk slowly I can see the abundance and the beauty in all this debris.

As I tip toe through the obstacles opportunities jump out at me. I find a beautiful piece of green sea glass. I find a purple shell, a sand dollar, and a starfish.

Each shell, each rock, each object broken or whole has its own story to tell. It has lived a lifetime, it has travel the sea. If I look and feel and listen I may learn a piece of its history.

In each piece that I notice, each piece that attracts me is telling me something about myself or my life. As I discover the beauty of the seashells I discover the beauty within myself and my life.

This Dance is one of slow and carefully planned movements. It is one where the feet must tip toe with dainty, tiny steps across the sand. It is one of extreme concentration and awareness, complete alertness. This dance is one of searching, finding, learning, and discovery.

Dancing in the Rain

Vulnerable in the rain that is falling from the dark grey clouds. Waves of deep purple, the ocean behind them dark green. The beach is deserted. Only crazy me, standing out here in gale force winds and pouring rain. Magnificent is the ocean in her raging glory.

The raindrops are the tears that I can't cry anymore. Anxiety clings like the clouds in the sky while I try to let go. Surrendering to the difficult situation, when you want desperately to make something happen.

Rain is another form of the water that we need for nurturing and growth. It cleanses away all sadness, grief and pain. All of our feelings are valid. Shedding the skin of them is a part of the process of life.

Each raindrop is part of the foundation of life. Collectively they create the lakes, rivers and this magnificent ocean. Rain clears us, heals us.

So Dance in the rain. Dance the teardrops. Each teardrop contains a pearl. And when the sun comes out after the rain it creates a beautiful rainbow.

This Dance is one of release, clearing and healing. Allow the rain to drench the skin and let it explode into disordered chaotic movement. Settling into soft mellow steps until steady and natural. Dance in the raindrops as they are liquid sunshine.

Dancing in the Fog

Fog obscures the island. The ocean is lost in the midst. The misty drizzle suits my mood. I stand here staring at an ocean I can't see.

I feel at peace out here in the fog. No one around can see me if they are even out here. I feel invisible now. I have felt invisible for a great deal of my life.

The ocean and sky are one. I feel the ocean as she slips over my feet. The mist is so heavy that drops of moisture completely dampen me.

I breathe and breathe again. Despite the damp fog I can feel the warmth on my face...warm wetness....I can't see anything in front of me, beside me or behind me...just this glorious moment.

I dance with uncertainty. Yet within that uncertainty I feel the Angels dancing around me....Mystical magic of spirit....The fog is magical as it makes all my troubles disappear.

Hidden in the fog is a perfect moment...a perfect dance. I don't need to see the past or the future. I just need to be dancing in the moment with the Angels guiding my steps.

This Dance is soft, subdued, and uncertain. Let
the fog drift around you and shadow you from
outside influence. Weave the steps through the
inner landscape to a place of total peace within.
Be comfortable with not knowing what direction
your steps are taking you. Trust your instincts
and keep moving.

Dancing under a Rainbow

Rainbows are beautiful, magical creations. They remind us that after a rain the sun shines with color. We realize that without the rain the sun cannot create this beauty.

Rainbows often arch across the island from the mainland to the sea.

One day as I was relaxing on the beach observing what was going on around me, I notice a rainbow forming in the sky, red, orange, yellow, green, blue, indigo, and violet. I watched the colors grow in intensity until they were so strong they became solid arches.

The arch of the rainbow stretched from the north horizon to the south horizon. I was dumbfounded that only a handful of people on the beach were aware of this captivating occurrence right in front of our eyes.

I was drawn to it. It called to me. I wanted to experience the bliss of being under it so I walked into the sea. I swam in the ocean underneath the rainbow.

It felt like I was in an enchanted body of water. I felt exhilarated yet serene. I felt like one of those mystical creatures in the Irish myths who could make anything happen. I almost believe that if I could swim to the end of the arch I would find a pot of gold.

Incredibly as I danced a second rainbow
appeared creating a bridge.

These breathtaking rainbows lasted for what
seemed an eternity as time stood still while I
danced under them in the ocean waves.

*This Dance is one of childhood dreams, fantasy,
magic, and feeling that anything is possible. The
movements are flowing, full of wonder and
delight. The steps are filled with exquisite,
fairy-tale charm and magic.*

Dancing in Joy

I can come to the beach disconnected,
restless, sad, angry, confused, and filled with
longing. Just one look out over the ocean, one
deep breath of sea air and I release the stress,
the restlessness, the sadness, the pain, the
anger and connect to the earth and to myself.

I am present in the beauty and all my thoughts
and all my heartache evaporate. I am light
hearted and nothing cam disturb or interrupt
this serenity.

I put on my music and skip, dancing, down the
beach. What a glorious day to be outside. No
matter what else is going on or not going on in
my life I can come here and commune with the
great ocean, feel the sand on my feet and be
at peace. Whatever time I spend here is
perfect. There is nothing wrong in these
moments.

Here by the sea I am home. I am in touch with
both my earthly connection and my divine
connection. I am in JOY.

I dance down the beach in a world of my own.
I drift off into a divine world. I dance into JOY
that oozes out of me from within...laugh if you
want to....that laugh might just let out a spark
of Joy within your soul.

Joy dances from within me to the surface of life. Creativity flows from the joy that races out of the waves of the sea to me as I dance down the beach, content in my being, in who I am and who I have been, and who I am becoming.

This Dance is one of light soft movements in large boundless movements. It is divinely connected and earth bound. The steps are pure enjoyment, no restrictions. Happiness spills into the steps, leaps, spins and twirls from Heaven to Earth. Dancing on the beach...Dancing in the Waves...Dancing on water....Dancing on cloud nine...

Conclusion

The wisdom of our hearts rises from the lessons of nature and takes wing in our creative expression.

I have become addicted to the ocean, to her beauty, to her colors, to her movements, sounds and rhythms, to the beach and her ever changing landscape.

I have made friends with the dolphins. I am in touch with my earthly connection, to the very breath of life. It feeds me and nourishes my body, mind, emotions and soul. It lifts my spirit. It gives me strength and courage. It provides solace, stillness and serenity. I am in Joy.

The ocean gives me life when I have nothing else. Without it nothing makes sense to me and nothing else matters. When my coffers are empty...when I am all alone...when I am overwhelmed...when I fall apart, this is where I need to be. One look at her and all my troubles are swept away. All sadness drains from my body. I am lifted by the wings of the waves. She reminds me of who I am and who I have been and who I am becoming.

The sand supports me, grounds me to the earth. The ocean relaxes me into the present moment and heals my soul. In this moment everything is perfect. My feet move to the sounds and rhythms of the waves and the song in my heart.

Dancing on the Beach is the way I express the depths of my love for the ocean, living at the beach and loving life. I am speaking a language that comes from the core of my being and expresses the gratitude and appreciation for all she does for me. I am living a dream that I have long waited for.

About Beach Dancing

I can never seem to just walk down the beach.
Being on the beach with the ocean at my side I
can't help but move to the sound of the waves.

My body moves to the delight of my heart and
the breath of my spirit. Whether the ocean is
softly glistening or roaring or calmly coming
ashore beside me her magnificence sparks the
delight within.

The ocean never ceases to charm me, to bring
a smile to my face, to exhilarate me. She
excites me like nothing else. It is thrilling to
get to communicate and interact with her
every day. She never fails to soothe me,
encourage me, and revive my spirit.

The only way I know how to express the
wonder, awe, gratitude, appreciation for the
privilege of experiencing all the beauty is to
move...

*The Dance Walk is one of skipping, twirls, and
arms flowing to the sky. It is walking to the
beat of the roaring ocean. It is stepping into
and out of the water as she glides up and down.
It is splashing and kicking. It is tip toeing
through shells. At moments the steps are slow
and the next they are gliding and the next they
are looping and spiraling along the shore.*

And Dance Walking turned into

Dancing on the Beach!

Dancing on the Beach is a combination of my passion and love of the ocean, beach and dancing. Being here at the ocean my soul cannot hold back, it must express itself with movement and dance. The ocean sings her own song that touches my spirit, entraining my body to move with her. Dancing is rhythmic movement brought to life by our bodies and spirit.

Beach Dancing is a unique and fun way to improve your health; mind, body and spirit. It is a combination of yoga, tai chi, ballet, expressive dance and meditation, enhanced by the fresh sea air, the water and the beauty of the ocean, sun and sky.

You are grounded with your bare feet in the sand, energized by the oxygenated air, relaxed into meditation by the rhythm of the waves, inspired by the ocean itself as you toss your inhibitions into the sea breeze. Your heart soars into bliss.

Set Yourself Free
Dance on the Beach

About the Author

Cathy Teoste is a writer and life coach focusing on women's identity and sense of self. She has a BA from Lesley University majoring in Holistic Studies. She went on to earn her MA Degree in *Holistic Health and Wellness.*

Life experiences awakened a passion for women's development, self-care, self-identity and authentic self-expression. Her passion for travel and the ocean have connected her studies to finding the wisdom within through the wisdom of nature and the word.

It is this unique combination of personal experiences combined with her education that makes her a compassionate, knowledgeable teacher and guide. Cathy walks the talk – in fact, she walks the life more than she talks- she teaches by example.

Cathy's love of the ocean sparked her to spontaneously start dancing as she was walking on the beach. She realized then that she had just discovered an important tool to Wellness; Mind, Body & Spirit and so Beach Dancing was born.

Cathy now lives on Topsail Island NC where she can be found dancing on the beach when she isn't in the ocean or sitting with notebook in her hand writing.